Animal Teams

Sea Otter Families

by Angela Lim

FOCUS READERS®

BEACON

www.focusreaders.com

Focus Readers is distributed by North Star Editions:
sales@northstareditions.com | 888-417-0195

Produced for Focus Readers by Red Line Editorial.

Photographs ©: iStockphoto, cover, 1, 14; Shutterstock Images, 4, 6, 8, 10, 12, 16, 19, 20–21, 22, 24, 26, 29

Library of Congress Cataloging-in-Publication Data
Names: Lim, Angela, author.
Title: Sea otter families / by Angela Lim.
Description: Mendota Heights, MN: Focus Readers, [2025] | Series: Animal teams | Includes bibliographical references and index. | Audience: Grades 2-3
Identifiers: LCCN 2023053997 (print) | LCCN 2023053998 (ebook) | ISBN 9798889981947 (hardcover) | ISBN 9798889982500 (paperback) | ISBN 9798889983590 (pdf) | ISBN 9798889983064 (ebook)
Subjects: LCSH: Sea otter--Juvenile literature. | Sea otter--Behavior--Juvenile literature. | Sea otter--Infancy--Juvenile literature.
Classification: LCC QL737.C25 L56 2025 (print) | LCC QL737.C25 (ebook) | DDC 599.769/5139--dc23/eng/20231213
LC record available at https://lccn.loc.gov/2023053997
LC ebook record available at https://lccn.loc.gov/2023053998
Printed in the United States of America
Mankato, MN
082024

About the Author

Angela Lim is an MFA student in poetry at Indiana University.

Table of Contents

CHAPTER 1

Ready to Rest 5

CHAPTER 2

Raising Young 9

CHAPTER 3

Clever Hunters 15

Healthy Oceans 20

CHAPTER 4

Staying Clean 23

Focus on Sea Otter Families • 28

Glossary • 30

To Learn More • 31

Index • 32

Chapter 1

Ready to Rest

A sea otter carefully **grooms** her baby. She licks its thick fur to remove dirt. She scrubs it with her paws. Next, she blows air into the fur. This makes the coat fluffy. It keeps the young sea otter warm.

Baby sea otters rely on their mothers for the first six months of life.

Many sea otters spend more than 10 hours a day resting.

The sun is about to set. The mother and her baby join other sea otters. Being together keeps them safe. **Predators** are less likely to approach a large group.

The sea otters rest together. The mother falls asleep with the young sea otter on her chest. She holds another otter's paw as they doze. The ocean swirls beneath the sleeping otters.

Sea otter mothers usually have just one baby each year.

Chapter 2

Raising Young

Sea otters do some activities alone. But they are **social** animals. Sea otters often rest together. They rest on the water's surface in large groups.

Eating and staying warm takes a lot of energy. Resting helps sea otters regain their energy.

Most rafts have at least 10 otters.

These otter groups are called rafts. A raft can have more than 100 otters. Otters in a raft link their paws. They drift together. That way, single otters do not float away. It helps keep them safe, too. They can all avoid danger together.

Rafts are usually separated by gender. But males and females come together to **mate**. After mating, females give birth to pups. Pups and mothers form strong bonds. Pups need their mothers to survive.

At first, pups can't swim. So, mothers carry their young on their chests. Pups can't find food.

Some sea otters rest wrapped in kelp.

The mothers help. They dive underwater. The babies stay on the surface. Their thick fur helps them float. But ocean **currents** could sweep them away. So, mothers wrap their pups in **kelp**. The kelp anchors the babies to the seafloor. When a mother is done finding food, she comes back up. Then she can unwrap her baby.

As pups grow, they learn skills from their mothers. Later, they can survive on their own.

Sometimes a mother can't care for her pup. When that happens, another female might raise the pup as her own.

Chapter 3

Clever Hunters

Sea otters eat many types of **prey**. Their diet may include sea urchins, crabs, and clams. They may also eat squid and octopuses. Sea otters dive to find their food. They swim down to the ocean floor.

Sea otters can dive as deep as 250 feet (76 m) before coming back up.

Sea otters have strong teeth. That helps them catch and eat prey.

Then, they bring their food back up. They eat it on the surface.

Sea otters often specialize in hunting certain prey. They go after only one kind of animal. Even otters in the same area might eat different foods. That helps all the otters. They don't use up one food source. As a result, they can all survive. And otters can find prey more easily.

Sea otters often hunt alone. But pups watch their mothers to learn. They learn skills such as storing food. Sea otters have loose skin under their arms. Storing food there keeps their paws free. Sea otters can grab more in each dive. They save energy by diving less.

Foods such as clams have tough shells. These animals can be difficult to eat. So, mothers teach their young what to do. A pup watches its mother float on her back. She holds a clam to her chest. Then she smashes it open with a rock.

Mother sea otters can pass their taste in food to their pups. When the pups grow up, they often eat the same foods their mothers did.

Sea otters eat the meat inside clam shells.

After learning, young sea otters can hunt and feed themselves. Later on, they can feed their own pups.

THAT'S AMAZING!

Healthy Oceans

Sea urchins eat large amounts of kelp. But many other ocean animals need kelp, too. They use it for food and **shelter**. Without predators, sea urchins could eat entire kelp forests. It would be hard for other animals to survive.

Sea otters help balance the number of sea urchins. Otters eat around a quarter of their body weight a day. That often includes many urchins. So, scientists track the number of sea otters. A large number in one area is a good sign. The **habitat** is balanced in that area.

Sea urchins come in many colors. Sea otters often eat purple urchins.

Chapter 4

Staying Clean

Sea otters can spend hours each day grooming. They use their paws, tongues, and warm air to get clean. They groom for several reasons. Grooming helps sea otters protect their fur coats.

Grooming can involve strong rolling motions and soft rubbing and licking.

Sea otters have the thickest fur of any animal.

Thick, healthy fur traps body heat. That keeps sea otters warm.

A sea otter's body also makes natural oils. These oils protect skin from cold water. Grooming helps sea otters spread the oils around their bodies. However, dirty water can make their fur dirty. And some oils are not useful. For instance, food grease can harm otters' fur. So, sea otters may need to groom after meals.

Sea otters often groom themselves. But reaching some areas is difficult. So, sea otters groom one another, too. Their grooming becomes a social activity.

Baby sea otters have thicker fur than adult sea otters.

Young sea otters do not know how to groom. Mothers must groom pups. That keeps the pups clean. It strengthens their bonds, too. Over time, pups learn grooming skills. They copy the behaviors they saw. Soon, they can groom themselves. Then they can help others in their raft. And they can keep their family healthy.

In the past, people hunted sea otters for their beautiful fur. Sea otters became **endangered**. They are still endangered today.

FOCUS ON

Sea Otter Families

Write your answers on a separate piece of paper.

1. Write a few sentences about why resting together helps sea otters.
2. Young sea otters learn many skills from their mothers. What skill do you think is the most important? Why?
3. What tools do sea otters use to break open shells?
   - A. rocks
   - B. kelp
   - C. fur
4. What could happen if an otter did not groom its fur?
   - A. It could get too cold.
   - B. It could starve.
   - C. It could dive deeper.

5. What does **anchors** mean in this book?

So, mothers wrap their pups in kelp. The kelp ***anchors*** *the babies to the seafloor. When a mother is done finding food, she comes back up. Then she can unwrap her baby.*

A. makes something sleep
B. holds something in place
C. helps something move quickly

6. What does **specialize** mean in this book?

Sea otters often ***specialize*** *in hunting certain prey. They go after only one kind of animal.*

A. to focus on one thing
B. to do something together
C. to gain lots of energy

Answer key on page 32.

Glossary

currents
Water movements that go in a certain direction.

endangered
In danger of dying out.

grooms
Cleans.

habitat
The type of place where plants or animals normally grow or live.

kelp
A large type of seaweed that grows from the ocean floor.

mate
To come together in order to have babies.

predators
Animals that hunt other animals for food.

prey
Animals that are eaten by other animals.

shelter
A place that protects an animal from bad weather or other animals.

social
Likely to spend time with other animals of the same type.